SERVING

WITHOUT

SELLING

RICHARD

BROCCHINI

Serving Without Selling

Richard Brocchini

Copyright © 2015 Richard Brocchini

Printed in the United States of America

DEDICATION

THIS BOOK IS DEDICATED to entrepreneurs, firefighters, service personnel, my family, and any and all who understand it's all about serving each other.

SERVING WITHOUT SELLING

FOREWORD

BY BRIAN SMITH

ON MY THIRD MORNING in America, I woke to smoke almost down to floor level in my rented house.

In my own book, I describe the terror I felt with my face pressed up to the bars on the window where I had punched out the glass in an attempt to try and gasp for air, while the smoke poured through the jagged hole over my shoulders.

When I heard the sirens in the distance, I knew I was NOT going to die.

That's how much blind faith we have in firefighters, since we "believe" they have the highest level of training, combined with courage and an amazing desire to serve the "customer" without question.

When Rich first asked me to write this foreword, I didn't see my relevance, as I had no firsthand knowledge of what it takes to be a firefighter. But, I was in for a treat when I read the manuscript.

I became intrigued by how similar the paths in starting a business as an entrepreneur and becoming a firefighter really were.

The years of unpaid study and training just to prepare for the entrance exam in the highly competitive field of firefighters seemed eerily like the long period of gestation every business needs to get traction.

Rich's comparison of the "customer service" instilled in every firefighter parallels the critical need to retain customers, no matter what business you are in.

The mantra to exhibit integrity and serve others as the greatest contribution a firefighter can make are exactly the same values that I employed in building the UGG business into what would become a billion-dollar brand.

Read on. You are in for a treat as you discover a blueprint to be happy, productive, and successful in whatever business you are undertaking.

Brian Smith

UGG Australia Founder

Keynote speaker and author of *The Birth of a Brand – Launching Your Entrepreneurial Passion and Soul*

FOREWORD

BY RONNY J. COLEMAN

MANY YEARS AGO, I told a writer friend that I was going to write a book. He laughed and said, "I doubt you will ever finish it." I asked, "Why?" His response was, "You are talking about writing, instead of writing ... writers put their thought onto pages with print; talkers put their words out in hot air." His point was that writing is permanent and talking is temporary. It was a challenge I could not refuse. I finished the book almost a year later and called him to get an apology. He responded by saying, "Anyone can write one book!" Since then, I have authored many books, but James Meidl's admonition still rings in my ears when I hear that someone is going to write a book.

That thought process, however, never entered my mind when Richard Brocchini told me he was working on his book. The reason is simple. He practices what he preaches. He is not just a talker, but rather he is a thinker and a doer, and definitely a writer.

This book reflects favorably upon two concepts. On one hand, it addresses why some people have dedicated their life to service. It also emphasizes how a skill set and creativity are important in the business world. He has done a masterful job of comparing the basic values of a public servant with that of an entrepreneur. He has demonstrated in this book that the values that drive service and sacrifice are closely aligned with those that improve upon the possibility of being a success in life as a business leader.

Richard has woven a tapestry of the skill sets needed to be successful in handling emergencies and those skills required to develop and sustain a successful business. His observations in comparing and contrasting these two worlds are practical, doable, and measureable.

As a former fire chief and state fire marshal, I take off my helmet to Richard for this effort. Now that I am retired and in a business of my own, I doff my civilian hat, as well. This book is an excellent effort that provides a common sense solution to making good things happen. My good friend, Jamie, passed on many years ago, but I know he would view this book favorably because it has been completed and it's not Richard's first. I look forward to many more to come.

Ronny J. Coleman
Retired State Fire Marshal

ACKNOWLEDGEMENTS

AS A FIREFIGHTER AND entrepreneur, I have been privileged to have been influenced by some truly incredible people. It is an honor for me to acknowledge my fellow firefighters and the many people who have greatly inspired both this book and my life.

Thank you, Greg S. Reid, for your continued support and mentorship. You have helped pave the path for my success and continue to give sound counsel that is priceless.

Thank you, Chief Ron Coleman, for your mentorship and being an outstanding leader for everyone in the fire service. The many ways you have influenced the fire service has enhanced the level of service provided to the public for generations to come. Your support is highly valued and very much appreciated.

I would also like to thank Lane Ethridge for his support and insight to share with an open heart.

Thank you, Brian Smith, for your kind soul, mentorship, and authenticity.

SPECIAL EDITS
Thanks to my Dad for his edits

INTRODUCTION

MY EXPERIENCE AS A firefighter and a businessperson has given me unique insight into the keys to success. In this book, I share an inside look into why firefighters are successful. Why? Because the way firefighters conduct business every day will carry over into success in any business. This insight has never before been shared—until now. Once you learn these fundamental, but transformational, principles, you'll be able to apply the same strategies to your success.

One of the first questions I'm often asked is how being a firefighter relates to being a successful entrepreneur and business owner. To most, the two careers are worlds apart. However, in this book, I'm going to share with you some of the insight I've gained from firefighting and how it is much more relevant to the business world than one would think. The truth is, the very characteristics that make a good firefighter can make anyone a great entrepreneur.

Firefighters have earned the respect and appreciation of communities and citizens ... and for good reason. *It's not just about what we do, but very much about how we do it.* You're about to learn the characteristics and traits that a firefighter must have when serving the community—the very same success strategies that will make you a successful business owner and entrepreneur. You see, most people have it all wrong. They think an entrepreneur must sell to be successful, when, in fact, the opposite is true. To be successful in business, one should serve, not sell. In this book, you'll learn not only why that is important, but how to implement this philosophy in your career.

As a firefighter and an entrepreneur, many people think I'm in a unique position. However, I can attest to the fact that firefighters very frequently hold other jobs or careers. There are many of us who are in the business of serving others and our community, while having an entirely different business or job during our "off" hours. Because I have the experience in both sectors, I've gained valuable insight in how they do, in fact, relate to each other.

INTRODUCTION

Whether you're a public servant or an entrepreneur, *being successful in business is never about sales—it's about serving.*

The one component that is most important in firefighting and business is service. Life and business mirror each other in many ways. In order to receive, one must first give. Only then will our dreams be fulfilled.

If your dream is important to you, don't give it less than your all ... and then some. Prepare for success. Invest the equity, time, labor, learning, training, and sweat in your business. And approach your business like a firefighter approaches his job, always remembering that success is not the result of what you do—it's the result of how you do it.

I hope you apply the insight I share in this book to your business. When you do, you'll approach your business with the one philosophy that is necessary for success:

Don't give up ... GIVE. Don't sell ... SERVE.

CHAPTER ONE

TRAINING FOR SUCCESS

THE START OF IT all...

I always wanted to be a firefighter, though my family often encouraged me to pursue other paths. "Be an attorney, be a doctor," they said. "You'll make more money." Like most people who are interested in firefighting as a career, money wasn't a factor in my decision. In reality, no one gets rich from fighting fires and answering the call for help. Our payment is larger than a paycheck; it's the reward that comes from helping people and knowing we make a difference in their lives. It's job security and the sense of belonging that is so common among members of a fire department and their brothers and sisters everywhere. The bond that exists between firefighters is one that cannot be denied, and it is one we must count on at all times.

Initially, I was under the impression that all it took to be a firefighter was wanting to be one. I quickly learned just how wrong I was. It all began on career day in high school, when I attended a session about firefighting. I was sure my life was going to change that day. All I needed was the desire and I'd be on my way! Nothing could have been further from the truth.

Have you ever thought about starting a business? You got all excited, thinking it would be easy. All you had to do was jump right in and your world would change! No more 9 to 5, no more bosses, no more working for the man. Finally, you would have the freedom to pursue your dreams ... and they would come true. If so, you're not alone. Many people underestimate the amount of preparation and work it takes to succeed. This is as true for firefighting as it is for business.

On career day, I learned that becoming a firefighter wasn't as easy as I first anticipated. If this was what I really wanted to do, and it was, it was going to require some prep work. I learned about a program called the Fire Explorers, which was a division of the Boy Scouts of America that was available to kids between the ages of 15 and 21. Luckily for me, one of the best in the state was located near my home. I signed up, thinking this was my in ... again, I was wrong.

This was just the first step of many and only the start of a lot of hard work, dedication, sacrifice, failing (temporary defeat), uncertainty, learning, training, and highs and lows I would experience. As a business owner or entrepreneur, that probably sounds familiar. I quickly learned that if I wanted to be a firefighter, there were hoops I'd have to jump through.

It would not be easy...

I couldn't just sign up and, voila!, I'd become a member. No, first I had to take a test to be a volunteer fire explorer. If my score wasn't high enough, I wouldn't get into the program and wouldn't receive the guidance and mentorship that I'd need to pursue my dream. Not wanting to fail, I sought information on how I could prepare for the test by asking current fire explorers about the testing process. They didn't have a clue who I was and really didn't have to help me at all, but they answered my questions and really tried to help me. *It's amazing what happens when you ask.* With their generous guidance, I passed both the test and the interview and was accepted into the program. The journey toward my dream was about to get real.

That's not the end of my story. It's merely the very beginning. Much like starting any business, it's never that easy. I was in the Fire Explorer program for three years.

During that time, I paid my dues and learned what it took to become a firefighter. I put in a lot of work, *all without pay.* I dedicated an enormous amount of time to learning, while holding a full-time job and going to school. Any social life I had ... well, it was non-existent, if you don't count socializing with my fellow Fire Explorers.

The same holds for being an entrepreneur or business owner. It requires action, education, training, sacrifices, and the very real need to surround yourself with the right people—people who are already doing what you want to do and are successful at it.

Moving on, one would think that I would be highly desired as a full-time firefighter after completing the Fire Explorer Program. Actually, I had to settle for being a volunteer firefighter, for two fire departments at the very same time. The truth is, firefighting is one of the most competitive fields there is. Qualifying requires a great deal of time, dedication, and hard work. In order to qualify, applicants must be 18 years old and have a high school diploma, or the equivalent, such as a GED. They also must complete extensive training and receive various certifications before they will be eligible. Before they can even enter training programs, they are required to take and pass three exams. First is a written test that covers many areas, including observation, spatial awareness, reading and comprehension, mechanical reasoning and ability, and memory. The second is a physical ability test, and the third is an aptitude test.

Only when they pass those three exams are firefighters eligible to pursue the application process, which often entails even more extensive training and certifications to increase their chances of being hired. The training is intensive and requires many, many hours outside of class studying and learning theory and practical assessment.

But that's not all. Many aspiring firefighters don't even attempt to apply for a position on a department until they've completed, and paid for, medical training that certifies them as an Emergency Medical Technician (EMT) or a paramedic.

That's just the beginning. After completing all of the training, firefighters have to put themselves through and, yes, pay for training at the Fire Academy. Only then will they even be considered as a qualified applicant for a full-time position.

The Fire Academy is an extremely extensive program. It is mentally taxing, fast paced, and physically grueling. On a daily basis, the body's physical conditioning and ability are tested to the max—without time to recover, you go back the next day for a more strenuous workout. Then, you go home, where you will complete tons of reading, knowing that even the smallest detail cannot be overlooked. The lecture and written portion of the program are so intense and comprehensive that it is often recommended that aspiring firefighters enroll in fire science classes before they attend the Academy to prep and provide them with sufficient background to succeed.

Many people believe that once they pass the Fire Academy, they can find a firefighting job anywhere, anytime. But for me, and countless others, there was just one more obstacle—firefighting positions are far fewer than the number of applicants. The field is very competitive. **I took 33 fire department tests before I was hired as a full-time firefighter.** That is not because I wasn't qualified—instead, it was because it is a fiercely competitive field. It is not unusual for a single department to receive thousands of applications for a dozen positions.

Does any of this sound familiar? Jobs are competitive in every industry. They require more education and training than ever before. Entrepreneurs and business owners are learning quickly that success takes more than desire ... it requires commitment, effort, dedication, training, equity, and unprecedented sweat. Even with those things, though, success isn't guaranteed.

You cannot expect to start a business and have the knowledge, expertise, and training to succeed on day one, any more than a firefighter can expect to know how to put out a forest fire, start an IV line, or perform CPR without learning what to do, what not to do, and then practicing it countless times. There is simply too much at risk to wing it and hope for the best.

Just like being a firefighter, becoming an entrepreneur is exciting. And like a firefighter, it is also dangerous. You invest your time, effort, money, and sweat equity into creating a lifelong dream. But if you don't approach it with the right knowledge, experience, and intense training, before long, you won't have the financial assets or mental desire to keep putting out fires—and that is precisely what you'll be doing. Without the right training, you'll continually be called upon to overcome mistakes. Sometimes, you might have to take several steps backward and start over—a process, by the way, which is very disheartening ... and one that can cause the loss of precious time when answering the call for service.

Treat your business like an emergency—like you're rushing to the call for lifesaving service. You don't want to stoke fires; you want to prevent them. You don't want to walk into your business green, without any training, education, or experience, just like you wouldn't want an untrained firefighter to answer your call for help. It is knowledge and training that prevents failure in any industry. Training for success is the key to success.

As an entrepreneur, take a look at your business. Are you prepared to give it your best at all times, under all conditions?

Ask yourself, "Am I trained and experienced in all aspects of running this business? If not, where am I lacking knowledge or experience, and how can I get it?"

Unfortunately, there are no qualifications for becoming an entrepreneur. There are countless positions open to anyone. There are no tests, academies, or programs that provide rigorous training that covers any possible scenario an entrepreneur may encounter. That must explain why so very few succeed. It's also why, like firefighters, entrepreneurs need to take it upon themselves to find an education, learn about their trades and businesses, and receive intense training *before* they consider themselves qualified for the most important job of their lives.

In every call, a firefighter has only one chance to get it right. There is no room for error. As an entrepreneur, you also might only get one chance. Train for your success and be prepared to prevent any fires that might come your way, instead of rushing to constantly put them out.

CHAPTER TWO

KEEPING YOURSELF ACCOUNTABLE

ONCE YOU'VE PUT YOUR heart, soul, and every ounce of curiosity into training so you are prepared for the many scenarios and situations you might encounter, you might think you're prepared to get down to business. Open your doors, launch your website, and you're good to go, right? Well, think again. Unfortunately, the first year of business is a testing period and the benchmark that many entrepreneurs use to gauge success—that's because only 50 percent of businesses survive their first year. Why is the first year such a big part of your success? Because it is during this time that you are maneuvering through the biggest learning curve you'll face.

Firefighters, no matter how well trained they are, must also survive that first and critical year. For firefighters, the first year is a probation period and a time when they could be fired for anything. Even the smallest infractions could result in termination. After all, for every firefighting position, there are thousands of potential applicants who might be able to perform their duties better, faster, and without error. To put it bluntly, new firefighters are dispensable—it is experience that makes a firefighter stand out from the rest.

Why is the first year tough? In firefighting, there is no room for error. Each mistake could literally cost lives. That's why there is no such thing as knowing too much or being "overtrained." Once a firefighter graduates from the Fire Academy, they find that the rigorous training and testing they've endured isn't over—it was simply a prelude for the intense training and constant testing that they will experience during their first year of probation.

As a new firefighter on the floor, we are put through tests every single shift, physically and mentally. We have to prove that we have what it takes morning, noon, and night—and that we have the motivation to do even more, if necessary. We are tested on a daily basis to see if we can handle the strenuous physical demands the job entails, and we are challenged with the necessity of learning how to overcome the mental and emotional intensity that is sometimes necessary in life and death situations.

As a business owner or entrepreneur, you are also tested every day. You aren't on probation, per se, but you are being tested—by your vendors and suppliers, your customers, your clients, your employees, your sponsors, your critics, and your competition. Every day, a challenge or an opportunity presents itself, and it is up to you to prove that you have what it takes to handle it appropriately and effectively.

Being faced with that level of scrutiny and examination, sometimes by others and sometimes by yourself, isn't easy. Slackers need not apply. As an entrepreneur, the only person who can hold you accountable for your success is yourself. Therefore, motivation is critical. Too often, people become motivated when push comes to shove—in other words, when they are already in trouble. Suddenly, they rush to learn what they're doing wrong or to put out fires that shouldn't have been started. A self-starter, on the other hand, takes it upon him or herself to be proactive and take whatever steps are necessary to keep their business alive, before it shows signs of struggle. This action is never more applicable and necessary than during the very first year.

In other words, don't sit back and wait for a fire. Prepare yourself for it. Have a back-up plan. Know what to do and what tools and strategies are available and how to use them. You might ask, "Why should I do something that I might not need to do?" I'll answer that question with another question: would you want a firefighter to answer your call for help who is not prepared or adequately trained for every and any possible turn of events? Would you want a firefighter who doesn't know how to respond to your situation swiftly or one who isn't skilled or confident in the use of their equipment?

As a business owner/entrepreneur you need to be a self-starter and must go all in. It's extremely important that firefighters be willing to go all in, especially because we are dealing with matters that have life and death consequences. Entrepreneurs, too, should treat their business like its life and death, which means to be fully committed. That's what the probationary period is for—it's a time to express your commitment and dedication, and to learn everything you possibly can.

Not only are first-year firefighters expected to increase their knowledge and skills, but they're expected to perfect them. In addition, they have to prove their level of expertise and abilities. Firefighters are expected to give presentations on equipment and policies to show that they know their company and product. They must know how to quickly don and correctly wear protective gear and use every piece of equipment in the department. They have to understand its capabilities, how to fix it if it needs repair, and how to use it in the dark when they aren't able to see. To gain that depth of knowledge takes commitment and self-motivation.

These test and presentations are like knowing your company and product. If you don't understand your company and product, you will fail. Entrepreneurs must know what they offer. You have to take it upon yourself to build that knowledge and understanding. It's a principle discussed by Scott Duffy in his bestselling book, *Launch! The Critical 90 Days from Idea to Market*. The steps one takes during their launch will ultimately mean the difference between success and failure.

Let's say you are in the process of launching a new product that you invented. That's great! However, you need more than a prototype to go to market—you need to do a lot of research. What are your product's capabilities? Do you know your product inside and out, and can you use it flawlessly with your eyes closed? Are you prepared to address questions and concerns with ease and confidence? Can you demonstrate every component and benefit of your product with ease? The first year of your business will depend on your ability and willingness to become a self-educated expert in your product and/or service.

Be accountable for doing what's right. Be accountable for what might need improvement. That takes motivation and commitment because as an entrepreneur or business owner, the only person keeping you accountable is you.

The first year is a year of learning how to be the best you can be. That pertains to more than your skills and understanding of your product or service, though. In other words, it's not just what you do and how well you do it, but the attitude that you express during every step of the process.

Again, it's about serving, not selling. You might think your success is hinged to sales, but in reality, your success depends on the service you provide to your customers. Are you pleasant? Do you dismiss those who aren't "sold" on your product/service? Are you courteous and willing to go above and beyond the call of duty to provide a solution to your customers and clients, while earning their respect and admiration?

When it comes to serving, attitude is everything. There is no component that is more valued and appreciated, yet so often overlooked in business. Firefighters with bad attitudes don't last long. There is always someone who will be eager and willing to step up and do whatever is necessary without complaining. In firefighters, this characteristic is so important that it can and has been the reason for termination of some fighters.

It is one's attitude that governs their ability to perform. Departments don't need negativity; they want people who represent their department and community in a positive manner. They want employees who accept any assignment—from washing a tanker to rushing into a burning building—without complaint. They need to know that every member of the department has their back and can be counted on at all times. If you don't want the job, all of it, someone else does.

It's not an easy task to stay up all of the time, especially when you come face to face with disasters, accidents, and people who are suffering. Sure, there are times when it's difficult to carry out our duties eagerly and with a smile, but it's also true that every task can be completed thoroughly, without complaint, and with the respect and cooperation that is necessary. This relates to business, as well.

Having a positive and cooperative attitude in business is vital. You are serving, not selling, and people want to do business with business owners who are pleasant and appreciate the opportunity to serve them. Your business cannot survive if you are dismissive or abrupt with your employees, customers, or vendors. The attitude you express in every business interaction, from obtaining accounts, selling your product or service, and even when addressing concerns or refunds, will frame your success. Just like a firefighter, if you aren't willing to perform all of your tasks eagerly and pleasantly, your customers can and will fire you.

Be objective and see yourself and your business from a customer's perspective. It's not what you do, but how you do it. People will always remember your attitude. They will remember how helpful and pleasant you are, how flexible you are, and the fact that you served them with a smile. When you are willing to go above and beyond the call of duty, people take notice. That's service that sells and produces the greatest and most valuable benefit to business owners there is—customer loyalty.

CHAPTER THREE

LEARNED BEHAVIOR AND REPUTATION

AFTER 9/11, FIREFIGHTERS FROM every corner of the country came to the scene to volunteer their services as a testament to their brotherhood and their unity. Images of firefighters flooded the Internet. The world saw them as heroes who were willing to sacrifice for their country in order to render aid to the victims and their fellow firefighters. Their actions in the wake of tragedy seeded their reputation with bravery, valor, and selflessness.

Firefighters are public servants and must maintain a positive public image at all times. Both on duty and off, they are subject to the scrutiny of the public at all times. What they say and do in public is a reflection on their profession and their department. In short, both off and on the job, firefighters must be vigilant about maintaining the public's trust and respect.

In regard to public service positions, people are more likely to remember the profession, not the individual person. Therefore, one person's actions can reflect on an entire department, profession, or an entire community.

In business, your reputation will also always impact your success. People want to believe they are doing business with someone who is honest, trustworthy, and reputable. If you're not, word will get out, and it absolutely will have an effect on your reputation and the reputation of your business.

This level of integrity and upstanding character not only applies to you, but also your employees. Like firefighters and other public servants, every aspect of your business must stand up to public scrutiny. Anything that can reflect negatively on you and/or your business will be used in developing the public's perception of whether they should or should not do business with you.

When it comes to the public's safety, trust is critical. The public has to be able to trust us with their lives, their property, their family members, and their safety. It is also true that the level of trust that is necessary extends between firefighters. We have to trust each other and know that every member of our department, and other departments, knows their job and is willing to do it. Any break in that trust or in a firefighter's integrity is a breach that fractures the entire department.

As a business owner or entrepreneur, you will also be subject to the scrutiny of the public. So will your employees and business practices. Your conduct in the community will impact your success on the job. While most people would like to believe that they can separate their personal and professional lives, it is very difficult to do. You are your business, and your business is you.

This doesn't mean that you have to have a perfect reputation. After all, nobody can please everybody all of the time. There will always be instances where we're subject to judgment, criticism, or ridicule, unfairly or not. There will also be times when we make mistakes; after all, we are human. On occasion, we err, usually unintentionally. The key to having an upstanding character and reputation is not to be totally beyond reproach, but rather to make every effort to conduct ourselves in an appropriate, respectful, ethical and honest manner whenever possible. It is not accuracy and perfection that earns public approval and admiration, but rather the way we conduct ourselves. There is a reason for the saying "conduct befitting an officer." By building a good public reputation, people are more likely to place their trust in us. When business owners have a good reputation, people are more likely to do business with them.

Firefighters, like businesspeople and entrepreneurs, are not perfect. They make mistakes and some have used poor judgment in their choices. From public intoxication to embezzlement, these errors create a violation of trust, not only in our professions, but in our community. A firefighter cannot do his job if he is not trusted with the public's safety and wellbeing, just as an entrepreneur cannot survive if he cannot be trusted by the community he serves. When one firefighter fails to live up to expectations, though, it tarnishes the reputation of all firefighters. The same applies to the business world. Look at the corruption and unethical behavior that has been exhibited by some on Wall Street. The behavior of a few has resulted in the distrust of so many.

Learning how to be an upstanding person who can withstand the public's critical eye is vital to your success. This is not something that comes naturally; an impeccable reputation is learned before it is earned. How? By learning from those who established the trust that is passed on to us. When we accept that torch, we must guard it, protect it, and keep it lit.

This is one reason why firefighters often associate with other firefighters. Not only are we in close proximity to each other for long periods of time while on duty, but we have to protect our reputation. The truth is, we always learn from and become like the people we associate with.

You've heard the saying that if one hangs with dogs, they'll get fleas, right? Well, the reverse is just as true. If you hang with honest, ethical, and upstanding people, you'll learn from them and benefit from their behavior and attitude. You'll learn how to be professional at all times. You'll learn how to be compassionate, considerate, and trustworthy. You'll align your morals and values to the people you choose to associate with.

A police officer isn't likely to associate with convicted criminals on a personal or social basis. It would create a lack of trust and respect within his department and community. It would also create doubt as to his loyalties. As a business person, you, too, should avoid associating with people who are not aligned with the morals and values you want to portray in your business.

Jim Rohn, an authority on success and personal achievement, said it well in his infamous quote: "You are the average of the five people you spend the most time with." Not only are you guilty of their behavior by association, but you also tend to model their behavior over time. For that reason alone, you should want to associate with people who are successful role models— people who have earned the reputation you want to have, people who are respected within their community and industry, and people who are willing to mentor and groom you to be an upstanding and stellar entrepreneur.

There is a reason firefighting is called a brotherhood. Just like relatives, we cannot pick our brothers. But we choose to associate with our professional brothers. It's a sense of unity and association that is tight, often not allowing those on the outside in, while keeping those on the inside from leaving the unit. The reason we are that tight is because we know, without a shadow of a doubt, that we can depend on these people, that they have integrity and have earned our respect.

As a business person, you need a similar team. You have to know that you can rely on them, just as they have to know that they can rely on you. Surround yourself with people who have earned the respect that you seek, learn from them, and model them. Sit in their audience and become their student. You'll find that it's not what they do, but how they do it that makes them stand out above the competition. In other words, how they behave is more important than what they do.

Have you ever walked into a restaurant, ordered a good meal, but had an unpleasant experience? The restaurant gave you what you ordered and your order came quickly, but maybe the server was short, abrupt and didn't seem to want to be there ... or the owner was loudly yelling at the staff, creating an atmosphere that wasn't enjoyable. That's an example of how behavior is more important than what you do.

In the firefighting industry, there are times when we have to do things that we don't really want to do. Maybe we'd prefer to be where the action is, but our orders are to stay behind and mop the floor. We are expected to carry out our duties without complaint. We could clean that floor to a mirror finish, cussing and complaining the whole time. While we might get the job done and do it well, it's not the quality of the job that we do that will be scrutinized by our brothers and sisters on the department, but the behavior we exemplified.

A firefighter frequently encounters people who are frightened, defiant, resisting, angry, and who have chosen vastly different lifestyles than most. While we cannot control the people and circumstances around us, we can control how we respond to them. We are expected to do our duties and care for them with professionalism, respect, and courtesy. Follow that principle in your business, and you'll find that it is your behavior and reputation that produce sales, not the product or service you offer.

CHAPTER FOUR

CONTINUED SUCCESS REQUIRES CONTINUAL WORK

EVERY CALL IS DIFFERENT. When the alarm sounds, a firefighter must be prepared and have the knowledge to address every potential situation. From rendering first aid to addressing a seemingly infinite number of health symptoms and issues, we have to know the best treatment to render in a moment's time. In the case of fires, environmental emergencies, and accidents, firefighters cannot take time to educate themselves on hazmat issues—that information must be stored in our minds where we can quickly and instantly retrieve it. This level of success can only be acquired through continual learning and continual work.

On-the-job training is vital for any profession, and the same is true for firefighters and paramedics. However, being able to do our jobs, and do them well, relies on dedication to learning more than we think we need to know and training for every imaginable scenario possible, however likely or unlikely it may be to occur. Arriving at the scene is not an appropriate time to learn how to put out a chemical fire or use vision equipment. This is work that must be done beforehand, and with rapid changes in technologies and equipment, we find that there is never a shortage of work or training to do to stay abreast in our trade.

Continued success requires continual work. A firefighter cannot put out a fire and declare him or herself to be a lifelong success, just as a business owner cannot hinge his entire business on one sale. Every encounter, transaction, and experience is different. Every client and situation is unique. Therefore, success can only come through continued effort, dedication, and learning.

Above all, a firefighter must be prepared to work, even when they are not answering the call for service. That works includes training, learning, practicing, improving, and making sure we're as prepared as we can be when the bell rings.

As an entrepreneur, are you prepared when that bell rings? Whether a customer walks through the door, telephones, or sends an email, do you have the answers they seek, the knowledge they need, and the skills to effectively dispel their doubts, concerns, fears, or reservations?

Success is not a one-time event that produces lifelong benefits; it is an everyday pursuit. While we can reap the rewards and satisfaction of success one day, we cannot ride on its waves for long. Continued success requires one thing, and it's the most effective contribution we can make to our success—work. While we'd all love to entertain the thought of sitting on a beach while money is pouring in and customers are multiplying by the thousands, that's highly unlikely here in the real world. The truth is, the minute we stop paying attention to our business, the less successful we will be.

Unfortunately, success usually takes longer than most people wish. They dive into it excitedly, gung ho to give it all they've got, just knowing that it's within their reach. However, it is easy to become disillusioned when the results they want don't come fast enough. This is one of the major reasons so many businesses fail within the first year. They give up, rather than working harder.

Greg Reid describes this concept in his book, *Three Feet From Gold*. In this book, he reveals what it really takes to succeed in business, as well as any pursuit in life, which is to stay on task, especially when obstacles present themselves. Success is a cumulative effort, and it takes commitment and perseverance. Equating it to a gold digger, as Reid does in his bestselling book, there are many who work very hard—they dig and dig and don't get the results they want. Their lack of success causes disappointment, and they ultimately give up. But the time when they give up is the time when they should actually work harder, because at this stage, they are closer than they've ever been to the success they've been striving for—they're only three feet from striking gold.

Firefighters understand this concept. They cannot quit and turn around when a fire presents obstacles—that is when they must explore other options and work even harder in their efforts to save and rescue. They must utilize all of the tools that are available to them in an effort to accomplish their feat. It is at this critical moment that we must choose between giving it our all and giving up. And in our industry, giving up is not an option.

Sure, it takes work. It takes mental and physical exertion, not just on the first day when we're pumped up and excited about undertaking a new career, but every day. Every day, firefighters are required to exhibit the same level of interest, commitment, dedication, and effort that we gave the day before. Any reduction in that effort helps to fuel the fires we fight, making them bigger, hotter, and harder to put out.

As an entrepreneur, you will encounter the same. However, for you, the fire is your competition. When your effort wanes, the competition is working feverishly to grab your customers and clients. It's improving and making progress, digging deeper and deeper, fanning the flames of success, while your success becomes stagnant.

This level of commitment and effort requires passion. You have to love what you do and invest in doing your best every day. As a result, you'll have the expertise to conquer any size or type of fire.

Firefighters must display expertise in all of their endeavors. We have to be experts in administering CPR, assisting accident victims, and fighting residential, commercial, brush and forest fires. The public expects that of each of us—nobody wants an amateur firefighter to answer their call for help. They want a seasoned veteran who knows exactly what to do in their time of need.

Of course, no one starts out as a seasoned veteran. That comes with time—and learning. Learning is a gift that lends itself to success, and it is how amateurs become experts. More than anything, it will not only help you put out fires, but it will be the key to preventing them from occurring in the first place.

The Fire Academy prepared me to enter my profession, but it didn't teach me everything I know. In firefighting, continuing education requires lifelong learning. We have to learn how to use new equipment, identify potential fire safety issues, address biohazards, and master innovative medical interventions and technologies. With each bit of knowledge, we increase our value to those we serve. And through lifelong learning, so can you. Embrace the opportunity to learn about the latest trends and technologies. Discover what today's demanding customers clients really want and familiarize yourself with the latest and greatest marketing strategies and tools. Above all, work on your personal and professional growth, for it is this investment in yourself that will build the foundation for your success. Through it, you will learn how to overcome obstacles, and even more important, you'll know how to prevent them.

Lifelong learning doesn't mean you have to earn a Ph.D. It also doesn't mean that you have to enroll in a certificate or degree program at your local university.

Lifelong learning is about knowledge and improvement—it's taking what you know to the next level. Yes, this type of growth can be found in a lecture hall, but there are other ways to tap into knowledge, such as mentors, training, and books. Attend events and seminars; read business advice penned by some of the most successful entrepreneurs and advisors; listen to audiotapes, and read books. Take away that which resonates and pertains to you and apply it to your profession and life.

I've become a student of books—books written by people like Greg Reid, who bases many of his teachings on the late and great Napoleon Hill. There is no shortage of self-help books available to entrepreneurs and business owners that offer incredible value—I encourage you to take advantage of them and the incredibly valuable training you'll receive from these experts who are willing to share their success principles and experience.

There are many individuals who only avail themselves of continuing education when it's mandatory. I can tell you, though, that bypassing such opportunities limits your capabilities and growth. I've witnessed firsthand the benefits derived from learning, especially in the case of volunteer firefighters who attend every training session possible—not because they have to or they're getting paid for it, but because they want to. They do it because their heart and soul are in their jobs and they want to be the very best they can be.

Of course, we all want to be the best we can be, especially if we're self-employed entrepreneurs. But yet, we will still make mistakes. If we're embarking on new territory or implementing a new philosophy, mistakes will be inevitable. If you're not making an occasional mistake, you're probably playing it too safe. There are risks in any profession, whether you are a firefighter or a business owner. Those risks are also part of the learning experience, and without them, there will be little growth.

The majority of people want to avoid making a mistake, and that's understandable. But know that mistakes are the greatest learning tool we'll ever have. They help us identify areas where we need additional training or knowledge, and they reveal areas where we can make improvements. It is through trial and error that we perfect our product or service. So many historical successes have found the silver lining behind each mistake or failure. As Henry Ford, who actually went broke five times before he became a sensational success, once said, "Failure provides the opportunity to begin again, more intelligently." Yes, mistakes are a priceless learning tool.

Mistakes will accompany our journey, especially in the beginning. It is our response to those mistakes, though, that will impact our growth and success. According to Confucius, "Our greatest glory is not in never failing, but in rising every time we fail." Thomas Edison was the poster child of this philosophy. After failing 1,000 times to create the light bulb, Edison eloquently stated, "I have not failed 1,000 times. I have successfully discovered 1,000 ways that do not work." With each mistake or failure, he knew he was one step closer to success.

When we first learned to walk, we fell down ... a lot. But through practice, and a few bumps and bruises, we mastered how to put one foot in front of another and walk. At the time, it seemed so hard to do, and it required learning how to do something we'd never done before, practicing it, doing it wrong, and figuring out how to get it right. Only then, were we able to successfully carry out the task with skill and ease.

The same holds true for anything in life. As a firefighter, we're dedicated to learning how to improving our skills and services. We strive to continually be faster, better, more skilled and educated. We work hard to perfect our skills so we can improve the quality of the services we provide. And we make mistakes. Those mistakes, though, reveal areas that need improvement, and rather than becoming upset about making them, we see them as an opportunity—an opportunity to discover ways to become even better in every phase of our jobs.

Work, learning, and mistakes are inseparable. You cannot have one without the others. Success relies on all three. Implement these three principles in your business, and like learning how to walk, over time, you'll be able to apply the lessons you learn without even thinking about it.

In a firefighter's profession, what we know and do not know can be the difference between life and death. As a business owner, what you know and do not know can determine if your business will survive. Work at it, train, read, and learn from your mistakes. Like the firefighter adage states, "Don't do it till you get it right; do it till you can't get it wrong."

CHAPTER FIVE

SERVING WITHOUT SELLING
(The Secret Sauce)

PEOPLE MIGHT WONDER ABOUT the logistics behind my philosophy: just how is it possible to be a successful entrepreneur if you focus on serving, but not on selling? Aren't sales the vital component of every successful business? Yes, in a sense, they are. However, it's not the actual art of selling that one should focus on. Instead, it's the art of serving. Master that, and the sales will come.

I call this concept the secret sauce—you know the one—that special sauce that makes something stand out over and above the competition. It's the component that makes you, your product, or your service different, and better than, anyone else.

As a business owner or entrepreneur, there is always competition. Even if you own the only Indonesian cuisine restaurant in town, you still have to compete against mom-and-pop diners, steak houses, fast food chains, pizza joints, bar and grills, and restaurants that offer Mexican, Italian, Chinese, or other cuisines. That competition is further amplified when you offer the same menu items as another restaurant.

Let's use barbeque ribs as an example. Many restaurants can offer fall-off-the-bone succulent ribs, so what makes them different? What makes a patron like one over another? The secret is in the sauce. It's the sauce that you perfect that no one else seems to be able to replicate that makes customers feel like they're getting a real treat. When the sauce is that good, it almost sells itself.

Those of us who are firefighters know there is no room for selling in our industry. Our roles are simply to serve—in any and every capacity we can. For us, the secret sauce is doing for others. There are no quotas or sales logs. Our business doesn't thrive by drumming up business. Yet, there is an expectation of performance and skill that is unparalleled and only shared by others who also serve without selling.

What is serving without selling? It's approaching your job or career without consideration for what's in it for you. It's approaching your position by asking what's in it for the customer or client.

I don't know a single firefighter who would say that he or she enjoys the risks and dangers of running into a burning building to rescue a life—although we wouldn't hesitate to do so when we're needed. Again, it's not about us—it's always about the people we serve. How can we reduce their pain or loss? How can we enhance or save their lives? Applying that principle to business means that you must always focus on the customer or client, never on your sales.

When you focus on sales, you're focusing on you, not your customer. When you focus on the customer, you're providing them with solutions, improving their life, creating positive experiences, and being of assistance when they want or need it.

Customers can sense when they're a number. They know when a business owner sees dollar signs. They have an uncanny knack for knowing when they're being sold to. They don't choose a business simply because it offers what they're seeking—they choose a business because of the way they're treated, how helpful the staff is, and how positive the experience is. In other words, when the business has that secret sauce, it's the special ingredient that makes customers come back time and time again.

Serving, not selling, affects so many aspects of a business, and it starts before a customer walks in the door and continues long after a sale is complete. It's the wedding boutique owner who has the uncanny ability to identify the most flattering dress style for a bride and whose recommendations woo her customers. To them, she is not selling them the most important dress of their life, but instead, she is making them feel more special and beautiful than they've ever felt. It's the restaurant owner who sits down and chats with an elderly gentleman who is dining alone and brightens his day. It's the insurance salesperson who reminds the couple with a new child that it's time to increase their life insurance by sending a personal congratulatory card or gift, rather than a form letter. It's sponsoring a Little League team and actually showing up to watch them play a game. It's about helping your customers and clients—not boosting your business.

It is serving, not selling, that actually attracts customers. Traditional sales methods are not as effective or as impactful as the relationships you create or the level of service you provide. Given the choice, customers will always choose to do business with an individual or company that puts them, not their bottom line, first.

Once you have those sales, your secret sauce will continue to work in your favor—even with dissatisfied customers. As firefighters, we know that we will do everything in our power to minimize damage or injury. But there are times when, despite our efforts, a fire cannot be contained and it results in total destruction. Even then, even when a homeowner has suffered immeasurable loss, they thank us. When you're an entrepreneur who does everything in your power to make your customers happy, even in those rare instances when it is not entirely possible, they will thank you. They will notice and appreciate your efforts—that's what they'll remember the most.

Those positive impressions and experiences create customer loyalty. That's because you're not only doing business with your customers, but you're also creating a relationship with them. No business can survive unless they build a relationship with those they serve.

The benefits of customer loyalty are invaluable. First, it's a well-known fact that it is less expensive to keep a customer than it is to find a new one. Marketing and publicity are expensive, and they're hit-or-miss. You never know what will work or what will bomb. On the other hand, you don't have to "sell to" a happy customer—they're happy to do business with you! And let's not forget that word-of-mouth advertising is still the most effective and least expensive advertisement you'll ever get. And it's your secret sauce that will help you get it.

Whether you call it serving or helping, it's all about relationships. When you focus on selling, the relationship is based on the sale, not the customer. On the contrary, when you focus first on creating a relationship, your customer will feel valued, which in turn will result in sales. The difference between the two is customer loyalty, which can be lifelong. You don't get that kind of loyalty from selling first because the relationship is based on the revenue and/or transaction, not the customer or client.

There is something infectious about helping others. We firefighters know that—it's easy to get hooked. Once you've experienced the internal rewards that come home from serving and experienced firsthand the impact it has on others and your relationship with them, you want to repeat it. When others see it, they, too, are enticed to help. At the most basic level, we want to make a positive impact on the people around us.

In Fayetteville, North Carolina, an 81-year-old Army veteran called 911 because he was hungry. Fighting cancer,

Clarence Blackmon had just returned home after spending months in a hospital and rehabilitation facility. With no family or assistance, and with limited mobility, he felt he had no choice but to call and ask for help. His request was that somebody, somewhere would go to the store and get him some food. He explained that he had the money to pay for it, but he didn't have the means or ability to get to the store. The dispatcher, Marilyn Hinson, listened. She wrote down every item he asked for: cabbage, beets, green beans, bananas, Pepsi, ham and popcorn. An hour and a half later, Marilyn and several police officers personally delivered the groceries. She put them away and made him a few sandwiches. To them, they were helping someone in need—they didn't need any thanks or repayment. What happened next? The generosity of these public servants was highly contagious, and donations and food for Mr. Blackmon started swarming in from across the nation.

Not only is helping others infectious, but it touches us at the deepest level and earns a level of unparalleled respect and admiration.

People around the nation were touched by Steve Wells, a Colorado farmer, who attended a police auction to benefit the survivors of fallen officers. Two brothers also attended, Tanner and Chase Brownlee, whose father was a deputy sheriff who had been killed in the line of duty five years earlier. The brothers were there to bid on their father's prized possession, *his former squad car. Tanner was quickly outbid by Wells, who purchased the car, valued at $12,500, for $60,000. Naturally, Tanner and his brother were disappointed—they had wanted this last piece of their father's legacy. Wells, though, had an ulterior motive. When he was handed the keys to the car, he turned around and gave it away, saying, "Tanner, here's your car." Everyone in the room was shocked and beyond touched. Tanner broke down in tears as he hugged his generous benefactor. There were few dry eyes in the room that day.*

Did Steve Wells want anything in exchange for his generosity? No. But did he get anything? Oh, yes. He got that feeling—that irreplaceable, one-of-a-kind feeling from knowing that he changed a life. He also got the instant respect and admiration of not just his community, but people across the entire country. I guarantee that if Wells had a business, it would have been bursting with customers after that. You cannot replicate the kind of feeling or the standing in the community that it created by focusing on sales.

I have created a blueprint of service for success based on this principle, which I call the Seven-Rung Success Formula. It's much simpler than any marketing or business plan you'll ever see.

THE SEVEN-RUNG SUCCESS FORMULA

1. Foster every relationship—every one of them is important.

2. Create ways to serve all of your clients, without trying to squeeze money out of them.

3. Always remember, it's not about you or your company. It's always about your client or customer.

4. Create an emotional experience for your clients/customers.

5. Think value before revenue. It's about how you can be of value to them, not how their business will benefit you.

6. Be authentic—hype is outdated. You don't need gimmicks and wacky promotions to stand out. Authenticity and sincerity make a greater impact and impression.

7. Have fun. Enjoy what you're doing and let people see it.

A fire department follows the Seven-Rung Success Formula. We don't need Sparky the dog or other gimmicks to create awareness or earn the admiration and respect of our communities. We simply serve others

65

every day. Every call, every patient, every family, and every house or building is just as important as the one before. We're not in it for the money—we're in it because this is what we truly want to do. We enjoy our jobs. The communities we serve know that—and they know they can count on us. By following the Seven-Rung Success Formula, your community will know it can count on you—and you'll earn their respect, admiration, and, yes, their business.

CHAPTER SIX

LIFE AND DEATH
CUSTOMER SERVICE

IF THERE IS ONE thing that is ingrained in a firefighter's psyche, it's that every situation has the potential to become a matter of life or death. From fires to automobile accidents, our first and foremost concern is to save lives.

Matters of life and death are always important, to us and the people we serve. It is in these situations that we know that any and everything we do or do not do could affect the outcome. So, too, is it with customer service in business. Delivering customer service in a life and death situation could give your business new life, or it could result in its demise.

Just what is customer service in firefighting? It's responding to the needs of the community in a professional manner. It's being timely and delivering everything we promise, and sometimes more. It's about being flexible and able to ascertain needs and adapt to them without hesitation. It's putting the community first, and making every call, victim, and family our utmost priority.

Every interaction you have with a customer is the same. That customer should be the most important customer to you at that time. It doesn't matter if they're window shopping, comparing prices, or have already bought a $30,000 car. When money has an effect on the way you treat your customers and the level of service you provide, you may find your business soon in need of life support.

The smaller your business is, the more critical it is that you deliver exemplary, stellar, over-the-top customer service. Big box stores and chains won't feel the loss of a dissatisfied customer as quickly as a small business owner. However, poor customer service has the potential to affect any business, large or small. Let's look at an example.

A husband and wife bought a new house, six weeks before their baby was expected to be born. They planned on getting new appliances quickly, the first of which was a washer and dryer. The best-laid plans, however, can find themselves falling apart. Their baby was born six weeks early, and now they had to move, had a very small preemie, and still needed to purchase and install appliances. They made a trip to a big box chain store, thinking it was well known and likely to stand by their products and service. A bonus—there was free delivery and installation. However, two things happened that changed their positive opinion. First, when they were paying for their items, the cash register would not let the sales clerk deduct the cost of delivery and installation. So a manager was consulted, who attempted to override the fees. It didn't work ... the first time, the second time, or the third time. While they were discussing how to circumvent the glitch, another customer approached with questions about another product. The manager walked away to assist the other customer. Really. Now, the sales clerk and the young couple were standing there, not knowing what to do. It was twelve long patient minutes before the manager returned. Twenty minutes later, the couple had a receipt in hand, showing they had paid thousands of dollars for several large items that were to be delivered and installed, at no additional charge.

Delivery was made on the date expected; but the dryer could not be installed. It seemed that the installers did not have the proper connections for their dryer vent. So the homeowners had to call the store to reschedule the installation of the dryer. Apparently, the crew at the house could not make the arrangements for this second visit. The local store transferred the homeowner to a call center out of state that handled installation schedules. The first date they could send someone out was seven days later, which was 14 days after the date of the original purchase.

The wife was on maternity leave and at home, waiting all day for the technician to arrive (any time before 8:30 a.m. and 4 p.m.). He arrived shortly after 3 p.m., but once again couldn't help them—apparently, the store had sent one of their television installers, rather than someone who could hook up the dryer. Well, of course, he also didn't have the proper connector for the dryer vent with him, either.

So the homeowner got on the phone again—this time, impatient and upset with the service they'd received from the first transaction until now. She was told that they could transfer her to the call center to reschedule the dryer installation. She rightly requested to speak to the store manager. The store manager said it was out of his hands; there was nothing he could do. But he did volunteer to transfer her call to someone higher up, at another center in another state.

Long story short, she was transferred five times. In the end, she was told they could not accelerate the dryer installation, and the soonest they could send someone out was in three days. Now, they knew they had a dissatisfied customer and, in order to make things "right," offered to send her a $100 gift card. She told them it was not about the money—this is true; it rarely is. It was the service that she was complaining about—and then she offered them a lesson in customer service. It goes something like this:

"I know about customer service. I work in customer service. I've been a store manager, and now I'm in healthcare—a field where patients can be very vocal when they're dissatisfied. What I keep hearing from your company is what you cannot do. If I took that position at work, I'd be out of a job. It's not what you can't do—it's what you can do. My job is to find a way to make it happen."

Well, as you can imagine, that spiel didn't change the company's policies. Nobody had the power to override any of them. But it gets worse ...

The homeowners asked if they could come in and pick up the part so they could install the dryer themselves. They were told they could, but they would have to buy the part—only their service team had the authority to install parts at no cost.

So, the homeowner suggested that maybe they should just come back and pick up the dryer. They were returning it—to which she was then told that it had been two weeks since the dryer had been purchased and it could only be returned if there was a defect. Any problems now would only be covered under the manufacturer's guarantee.

"How do I know if the dryer works? I can't even turn it on," she informed.

The homeowner then went to a small family-owned store, bought the necessary part, and installed the dryer themselves. It was that family-owned store that received their business when they were ready to replace their dishwasher, stove, and refrigerator—proving it's the service, not the sale, that influences customers the most.

When it comes to customer service, policies are made to be broken. But in this instance, the big box store had grown too big to care about one customer or losing their loyalty. They were focused on limiting costs, rather than generating satisfied and happy customers.

What would a firefighter have done in this situation? Well, hypothetically, a firefighter would have treated it like a third alarm. They would have arrived at the house quickly (sirens and lights fully activated), looked at the dryer vent, said, "Ma'am, I don't have the proper part, but I'll be back in a few minutes with it and we'll get your dryer hooked up this afternoon." A firefighter would have come back after business hours, if necessary, given the homeowner his or her personal number to contact if there were any questions or problems, and probably would have cooed a bit and asked to hold the baby. We really like babies.

And then the firefighter would have called the next day to make sure everything was working okay and to ask if there was anything else they could do—and we'd remember once again to ask about the baby.

This situation certainly wasn't life or death. But I think you can see that this situation could be life or death for a small business that depends on every sale to stay alive.

Customer service can be life or death to any business. Word of mouth is the best ... or the worst ... advertisement a business can possibly get. As firefighters, we are often the recipients of word-of-mouth advertising. People often comment to others or thank us publicly and personally, complimenting us for our professionalism, for going above and beyond, for giving it our all—even if the outcome was not the one that was desired. Again, it isn't the outcome that they are ultimately thanking us for—it is our "service."

Customer service is a part of every company, whether it is a retail store, restaurant, carpet cleaning company, dental office, or lawn care service. Depending on the quality of that service, a company will either thrive or die. In this day and age, with the power of the Internet and social media, good news travels farther, while the tales of dissatisfied customers are heard louder, longer, and can spread faster than wild fire.

While something may seem trivial to you, the business owner or entrepreneur, every situation is important to the customer. To them, even the smallest detail can leave an indelible impression.

Let's not neglect the fact that you never know what is going on a person's life. A small gesture of kindness to someone who is ill or having a bad day, or week, can make a difference. Going out of your way to say "you matter" to someone can go a long way toward earning their business and approval. That is true if you own a grocery store and your customer is purchasing a pack of gum, or if you own a car dealership and your customer is buying an SUV. How different would our homeowner's experience had been if only someone had promised to correct their mistakes and sent someone out with the right part to install the dryer the very next morning? I'm guessing, but I really believe that the homeowner would have not only felt like they mattered, but they'd also be grateful. When someone is grateful for the service you provide, you're truly serving without selling.

The service segment of our business *is* our business. It doesn't matter what we sell or do, if our customer service is dead, our business will die. Ask any customer why they won't do business with a particular person or company—nine times out of ten they'll say they had a bad customer service experience. Policies are often the biggest pitfall. Sure, they have a purpose—but when they stand in the way of doing something that is within reason, and even common sense, they can and should be bent or broken.

The customer is always right. We've heard it time and time again. Is it true? Not always, but in the customer's mind, you can bet that they think so. The big box store that sold the dryer might have thought this customer was a drop in the bucket and that their expectations were unreasonable. And it's also true that the customer might have been willing to patiently wait if their circumstances were different—if they didn't have a newborn, a new house, and so much on their plate at the same time.

Customer service isn't solely reserved for customers. It involves everyone you come into contact with, including vendors, delivery services, postal workers, employees, next door neighbors (yes, your relationship with neighboring businesses), and the entire community. Customer service is seeing how your business is viewed by everyone—from the outside curb appeal and cleanliness, to your hours of operation, to the ease in which sales personnel, delivery men, and postal workers can access you in order to do their jobs. It's about more than your company—it's how you and your personnel represent your company in the community. Are you upstanding members who are willing to volunteer and be involved in local events or planning? Are you willing to host an event or chair a committee? Do you support schools or local charities? Can your community and customers count on you, just the same as you count on them?

That's service without selling. People know they can count on firefighters. When they need us, all they have to do is call and we'll be there, ready to give 100 percent for them. Can your community and customers say the same for you? Don't wait until it's a matter of life or death—

breathe some new life into your business by empowering yourself and your employees to focus on what they can do to create satisfied, loyal customers—not on what they can't do. With impressive customer service, you'll eliminate the need for life support. As they say, prevention is always the best medicine.

Or as they say in the firefighting industry, only you can prevent forest fires.

CHAPTER SEVEN

MENTORSHIP

"WHEN THE STUDENT IS ready, the teacher will appear." Those words have had a resounding effect throughout centuries. We all need to learn—from books, teachers, and experience. But there are times when the greatest teacher we will ever have in business is a mentor.

What is a mentor? A mentor is someone who has already had success doing something that you want to do and is willing to share their wisdom and experience with you. Think of a mentor as a personal success instructor. It's kind of like Donald Trump agreeing to provide you with personal assistance in becoming a millionaire.

Mentors talk their walk—they teach you the things they learned throughout their career and life. These are things that you'd normally take years, even decades or longer, to learn … the hard way—through trial and error.

Mentors aren't reserved solely for entrepreneurs and business owners—many people have them. Firefighters have mentors—they are veteran firefighters who have amassed a lot of experience, those who climbed the ladder, so to say, to the upper ranks. They are fire chiefs, lieutenants, and fellow firefighters who are willing to cut the learning curve so cadets and new firefighters are equipped with their knowledge and experience much more quickly.

But let's not overlook some major benefits you can receive from mentorship that can be of greater value than knowledge and experience. Those are support, encouragement, and guidance. In fact, the benefits of mentorship are so great and conducive to long-term career success that many departments and academies have established mentorship programs for new recruits. Not only do mentors show them the ropes, but they also:

- Act as role models, providing one-on-one support and encouragement
- Are available to answer questions
- Help recruits through the hiring and/or promotional processes

- Make new firefighters feel included, like they are part of the network
- Provide guidance, assistance, advice when needed
- Prepare their mentees for success

Every fire department knows that its success depends on the success of each of its firefighters. We work together—as a unit—to create that level of success. It's not an each-to-his-own environment. We know that the stronger and better prepared each firefighter is, the better we all are.

As you can see, mentorship is a tool that benefits both new recruits and veteran firefighters. It's one of the reasons we are a brotherhood—a unit that looks after each other. Through mentors, we gain insight, advice, and on-the-job experience that cannot be gained through fire academies, college, or other avenues.

What is a mentor to an entrepreneur? A mentor could be a successful business owner who is willing to share his successes and lessons he's learned that will accelerate your success and lessen your mistakes. A mentor could provide an overview or detailed information in just one area. They might meet with you in person once a week or twice a year, or be accessible only via email or telephone. Whatever role they play and however they carry them out, mentors have contributed to the successes of many entrepreneurs and business owners for centuries.

- Steven Covey is a mentor to motivational success guru Brian Tracy
- Andrew Carnegie mentored Charles Schwab
- Robert H. Boyle mentored Robert F. Kennedy Jr.
- Warren Buffet was a mentor to Donald Graham (publisher, Washington Post) and Michael Lee-Chin (CEO, AIC)
- Hockey player Bobby Orr mentored Dr. Robert Thirsk
- Oprah credits Barbara Walters as her mentor
- Frank Sinatra's mentor was Bing Crosby
- Henry Ford had a mentor—Thomas Edison

What do these individuals have in common? They are all famous successful entrepreneurs, and they each credit their mentor as a part of their success. As you can see, even those who are already highly successful have mentors on their team—people who can help them go further and learn more as they strive toward new goals and pursuits. Henry Ford believed in this philosophy so much that he founded The Henry Ford, an institution that originally served as a school and was based on Ford's premise that the genius of some of the greatest people was not taught in textbooks. Today, it holds a school, as well as a display of innovations and resources that serve as a history of the finest minds and contributors to our country's progress. One could say that Ford made it his legacy to serve as a mentor to our country, even long after his death.

Because a mentor is such a powerful asset to every aspiring entrepreneur, I encourage everyone to find a mentor to accelerate their successes and reduce their failures. Learning from someone who knows what works, what doesn't, and the best practices to implement in business brings an arsenal of knowledge that cannot be replicated elsewhere.

Where do you find a mentor—someone who is willing to give their time and share their experiences and knowledge with you? There are many places. First, look toward other entrepreneurs, people who are already successful doing what they love to do. This person doesn't have to be in your industry—Henry Ford's mentor knew nothing about automobiles, but Edison certainly did know a few things about success and business. This individual could simply be someone who has successfully launched a business, or someone who has taken a business and turned it into a conglomerate. It could be a banker, an accountant, or a vice president. It could be an individual who has broken records in network marketing, or even a professional who you've admired for the way they conduct themselves and interact with the community.

To gain the most benefit from the experience, however, it is best to find a mentor who is a business owner or entrepreneur, for he or she will have the experiences and background that are relevant to you. Here are a few ways to find mentors:

1. Look in your own circle, or as we say in our industry, in your own department. Look for someone with experience who is supportive and willing to offer you guidance.

2. Relatives can be mentors, as well. Seek those who have the qualities you're looking for and who sincerely support your success.

3. Refer to social networks like LinkedIn, a good business resource, Facebook, or Twitter. There are reasons you are connected or have become "friends" or "followers," and many of them are because you look up to or admire these individuals. To enhance your efforts in this endeavor, support them, comment, ask occasional questions, and genuinely express interest in their thoughts and opinions.

4. Attend networking events where you'll meet other entrepreneurs and business people.
5. Join clubs or organizations that cater to the interests of the people you want to meet and know.
6. Attend seminars and workshops where you'll meet a variety of people from all industries and walks of life.
7. Books are fantastic mentors. They provide a plethora of information and guidance on virtually any subject. Knowledge is a wonderful tool that is so often undervalued. Don't forget books by inspirational and motivational authors, for their words, advice, and encouragement are just as powerful in your future success as industry-specific advice. When you feel your motivation begin to wane, books by inspirational figures like Greg Reid, Brian Tracy, Zig Ziglar, Les Brown, and Tony Robbins will light you on fire and get you back into the game.
8. Join a mentorship website, where you can request a mentor or volunteer to serve as one.

The FDNY implemented an experimental mentor program for new recruits who were about to enter the academy. Firefighters volunteered to mentor aspiring firefighters through the grueling physical training and the written and physical exams. Having someone who had been-there-done-that available to answer questions and tell them like it is was extremely helpful to the new recruits. While they did provide real insight on what to expect and the best ways to prepare, most reflected that it was the support and encouragement they received from their mentors that enabled them to successfully complete the program.

Having an individual or a team who will cheer you on when you need encouragement or applaud you for your successes is an invaluable benefit from mentorship. This was the case for Melissa Larson, who joined the Rockdale (Georgia) County Fire Department. Melissa's mentor wasn't assigned or selected because of experience, although her mentor was very experienced. Quite fittingly, Melissa's relationship with her mentor was the result of one fact—they were both females in a male-dominated profession. Juli Moncrief had a 24-year career in fire suppression, and like Larson, had started her firefighting career while raising young children. During rookie school, which encompassed eight weeks of intense training, there were days when Melissa was exhausted and didn't think she could go on. It was Juli who continually gave her pep talks and told her, "You've got this. Keep at it."

With that kind of support, even when you think a two-and-a-half inch hose is going to kick your butt, you find the strength and the will to dig your heels in a little deeper and find that you had what it took within you all of the time. You just needed someone to help you pull it out.

There is yet another type of mentorship that is emerging, known as reverse mentoring. It's untraditional, but given the diversity in skill and experiences among pioneer firefighters and rookies, it has real merit. Reverse mentoring switches the roles of mentor and mentee; in other words, it is the young rookie or recruit who mentors veteran firefighters and officers.

Don't mistake a mentor for a supervisor. A mentor is not—a mentor is an adviser and a supporter—which is precisely why reverse mentoring works.

How does it work? In reverse mentoring, it is the young, new firefighter who advises the older, more experienced one. Of course, this doesn't pertain to hands-on firefighting techniques and strategies, where experience is an enormous benefit. But it does maintain an open perspective that a younger generation has specific skills and experiences that previous, older generations might not. The following is a great example.

A large fire department had been researching software for its fire prevention division, but after a year, still hadn't found a program that fit its needs. After spending a great deal of time and making several purchases that fell short, they were frustrated. A new firefighter, still on probation, overheard several high-ranking officers having a conversation centered around this frustration. While trying not to step on anyone's toes, the rookie volunteered some information—it just so happened that he was a software engineer and designer in his previous job. "I could write that program for you," he offered.

They took him up on it, letting him lead the team. In the end, he created a program with every feature they wanted and even suggested some more. But that's not all—he mentored them, showing them how to use the program and its features and how to maintain and upgrade it.

Technological skills like these are second nature to many young adults who grew up using technology, while previous generations don't have that level of experience. Reverse mentoring is perfect for situations such as these, especially with the new technology that firefighters must continually learn as advances are made in computers and equipment. Regardless of our age or years of experience, we all have something that we bring to the team—reverse mentoring and traditional mentoring allow us to share that with others.

We can all see how one can benefit from having a mentor, but what's in it for the mentor? What does he or she get for their time, effort, guidance, support, and experience? Trust and respect are just two benefits. But there's something more. Greg Reid said it well in his book, *The Millionaire Mentor,* "The greatest success you'll ever know is helping others succeed and grow."

True, mentoring is usually voluntary; there is no fee or income for your contribution to another person's success. But it does contribute to your success, standing in the industry and/or community, and your legacy. Being privileged to be able to make a difference in someone else's career or life, to share your experiences, and offer your support is one of the greatest compliments you'll ever receive. It's also one of the most rewarding experiences you'll ever have.

I encourage each and every young entrepreneur to include mentorship in their business and career plan. Then, when they, too, become successful and are able to make a positive difference in another, it is my hope that they serve others by becoming a mentor. When you use your gifts, talents, and experience to help others, you're much like a firefighter. It is at that stage of your success that you are, indeed, serving without selling.

CHAPTER EIGHT

STORYTELLING

AH, THE GIFT OF GAB—not everybody has it, but everybody who does have it knows that it's not just a character trait, but also a very valuable business and success tool.

People have been telling stories since the dawn of time. Stories help us relate to others and give us an opportunity to experience a thing or event without actually having participated in it. I'm not talking about stories like the "fish that got away"—that's story telling at its finest, but also an exaggerated fictional tale. When I refer to storytelling, I'm talking about a way to relate an experience or a thing to others in a way that is appealing, relevant, and brings them a new perspective.

Imagine just how much more effective it would be to share a story about how a product or service benefitted someone, or even changed their life, instead of simply spieling off its features. Features are often depicted in brochures or product and service data sheets, FAQs, etc., and it's no secret that, while those marketing tools have a use, they aren't entertaining reading. Stories entertain. They pique our curiosity and emotionally appeal to us. In addition, stories bring a personal aspect into business that helps people envision how those features can make a difference in their lives.

We all enjoy a good story—we love to hear about people overcoming odds and accomplishing goals. People like to connect and relate to each other. They like to share. They like to participate and contribute. Firefighters are no exception. We share stories about our home lives with each other, talk about where we've been and where we plan to go. We share our plans and ask for opinions. Our experiences are part of our camaraderie, and the support, advice, and encouragement we give and receive by sharing and listening to each other's stories are beneficial in what we do. It's not uncommon to hear firefighters rehashing the details of a call or sharing them with the next shift when it comes on duty. Through these stories, we not only connect with each other, but we also receive valuable information that helps us as we conduct our duties.

The best stories in business are those that are compelling. They help the listener relate and emotionally connect to the story and the storyteller. And they are far more effective than hype or gimmicks. If there is one thing that your audience can detect, it is insincerity. People can see through hype—it's that transparent. Stories, on the other hand, bring a message to life, where people can envision them and even experience them.

Are stories an effective way to gain exposure? Yes. Can they help others identify with you or your business? Absolutely. You might attract some people if you hold a sale and advertise that a clown will be giving away free balloons, but they're coming to you for the wrong reasons. How much more effective would it be to share a story that touches their hearts, or one that inspires them to buy your skateboard so they, too, can experience the feeling of mastering awesome maneuvers like the four guys who awed them in your video? I can tell you that a video that tells a story is much more persuasive than an advertisement with pictures, prices, and features.

If you want to create change, tell a story. If you want to sell a product or service, tell a story. A well-woven story is the best and most effective form of marketing and advertisement. Why? Because stories evoke emotions, and emotions sell.

Jack Daniels uses stories in their marketing to relate the history and mystery behind their brand. They take the viewer to scenic Tennessee, where it all began, and depict the origin of the product in such a way that people resonate with the man who founded it and its historic and unlikely success, rather than seeing their products as just a bottle of whiskey.

Above all, by including a story in your business message, you have the incredible opportunity to serve others. You're not only feeding them information, but you're impacting their life. Charity: Water is one example. Their campaign to bring clean drinking water to all people around the world involved a compelling story. By transferring their cause to New York City and showing its residents carrying buckets of dirty water from ponds to apartments, they were able to make their viewers imagine what it would be like to be without a necessity that we take for granted. Through this emotional story, they have significantly increased their fundraising efforts.

Today, people don't just do business with a person or company, they are connected to it. In the past, businesses talked to or reached out to people, but it was a one-way street. With social media and the Internet, however, people now have the opportunity, and are encouraged, to communicate and interact with businesses. By "liking" a business on Facebook or following it on Twitter, they become part of its community and that business becomes part of their story as they share it with others.

Remember the ice bucket challenge for ALS? A nonprofit organization invited the world to connect and communicate with them by sharing videos of themselves dumping freezing cold water on their heads. All for a good cause, it raised more than $100 million dollars! What a story! And each video of someone participating the challenge was a story in itself. You cannot get those kinds of results or exposure from a commercial, advertisement, or plea—you get it from creating an emotional appeal, connection, and the freedom to interact and participate with a cause or a business.

Kickstarter is a great example that shows the impact storytelling has on results. Not only are people encouraged to tell their stories on the site, but they are required to do so. And it's been proven that the best stories are the most persuasive and produce the best results.

For example, an individual is using Kickstarter to raise funds for a cause that is near and dear to her. In this case, the individual's name is Annie and the cause is once again ALS, otherwise known as Lou Gehrig's disease. Now, Annie could try to entice people to donate to her cause by simply stating that she's trying to raise funds toward finding a cure and that she has a $1,000 goal. But then people wouldn't know the whole story, and she'd probably raise some money from people who already know her, but she'd fall short and wouldn't reach anyone outside of her circle.

What is the whole story? Well, it goes something like this:

Annie was just nine years old when her mom was diagnosed with ALS. Her mom, an active person who loved nature, was also Annie's best friend and role model. Throughout fourth and fifth grade, Annie watched her mom's health deteriorate until her once vibrant mom was confined to a wheelchair and eventually needed a feeding tube. Annie's childhood, naturally, was a sad and traumatic one, and became even more so at the age of eleven, when her mom lost her battle. Annie spent the next ten years of life learning about the disease and finding ways to support and spread news about research. Today, she has a college internship with a not-for-profit ALS foundation.

Her story is much, much bigger than saying, "I'm Annie. Please help me reach my goal and raise $1,000 to find a cure for ALS." By telling her story and sharing it with others, Annie would have the ability to tap into the emotions of others and appeal to them as the child of a victim of the disease. She would reach them at the deepest level and evoke compassion and sympathy from her audience, and she'd also become more real to them. Through effective storytelling, she could deliver her message and her plea and receive an astounding response.

Firefighters know that storytelling creates a response. We employ storytelling in the delivery of many of our services to the public. For instance, we attend grade schools and teach fire prevention and safety, often adding a story in our presentation to enhance our message and make it personal and applicable to their lives. Even children relate better to instruction that is delivered in the context of a story, rather than being taught via lecture and memorization.

The Peoria, Arizona, Fire Department (PFD) recognized that storytelling has value in a project submitted to the National Fire Academy in June, 2006.

The purpose of the project was to propose that storytelling was beneficial and had merit, so much so that the Academy should teach storytelling and make it required learning. At the time, the PFD was growing at a rate that caused concern that important customer service and leadership lessons were not being shared with younger generations of firefighters. The larger the department grew, the less opportunity there was for officers and senior firefighters to share their valuable stories with new recruits. Compounding the department's growth with the fact that a large number of veteran firefighters and officers were expected to retire in the near future, the department faced a huge loss—the loss of institutional memory.

There is no denying that firefighters love to share their stories—and the fact that stories put faces and interest on experiences and lessons. But by recognizing the fact that stories drive a message home better than "instruction" or "lecture," they are equipping their department and its members with experiences and lessons that have more longevity and impact.

People love to hear stories, whether it's around the dinner table, at the water cooler, or at the local pub. Stories mesmerize and pull them in—while other forms of communicating a point are dry and uninteresting.

That's because stories captivate us and make us feel. They make us think and have greater retention value than rattling off statistics, sharing instructional strategies, and touting formal backgrounds.

Nike is an example. I'm sure there are people who have visited Nike's website and/or read their "About Us" and historical background. It's probably safe to say that only those with the most retentive minds can recall that information. However, those who heard the "story" about the innovation behind Nike shoes aren't likely to forget it.

The story goes…

Nike was a shoe manufacturer that was struggling in the early 1970s. They certainly weren't slated to be the best or most popular athletic shoe brand, and no one expected them to be anything more than a small brand. But when the University of Oregon installed an artificial surface track, Nike went to work, striving to create a shoe without metal spikes that would grip the surface. Bill Bowerman, one of Nike's scientists and innovation engineers, struggled with the concept for a while. Then, one day while his wife was making waffles for breakfast, Bowerman had a bit of a brainstorm. Maybe, just maybe, the waffle-like surface created by the waffle maker would work! So he went into his lab and poured rubber into the waffle maker, thus producing the sole that has become the hallmark of Nike's success back in 1974. The shoe? Well, it was fittingly named The Waffle Trainer, and it is this shoe that launched the new brand that made Nike the icon that it is today.

People who hear Nike's success story rarely forget it. Why would they? It's unique and unforgettable! Success stories like that are not reserved for big brands; remember, Nike was a small-time shoe manufacturer, but they had a story long before they enjoyed mega success. Every person and every business has a story. Every foundation and organization has a story. Every firefighter and police officer has a story. It's the story that captivates and captures attention. Nobody wants to hear what Nike's shoes are made of, but nearly everyone loves to hear how they were invented. Nobody wants to hear technical data that bores them to death—they want to know *what does this mean to me? How will this affect me?* With a good story, they'll not only learn the things they want to know, but they'll find themselves wanting to know even more.

Have you ever heard a great story, and when it was over, you wanted it to continue? You asked questions, interjected opinions, and even dared to propose, "Wouldn't it have been great if ..." or "I wonder what would have happened if..." and sometimes, "Tell me more!"

That's because compelling stories involve the listener. The listeners becomes part of it, or at least they want to. Even more, stories entice discussion and participation—two things that traditional messages and sales methods do not invite or encourage. People don't want to do business with a person or company in order to be part of its success. They want the person or company they're doing business with to be part of their success. So before they invite you into their lives, their problems, and their needs, they want to hear your story.

Storytelling in business puts a face on your brand; it gives it life. People don't want to know what you do—they want to know why you do it, who you do it for, and how you do it, and what it can do for them. A well-crafted story will pull them in and help them make a decision long before they know they've even made it.

For example, there were severe storms recently across the Midwest. High winds toppled trees and power lines, creating a headache and massive cleanup for homeowners. A couple lost an 80-year-old maple tree, the majority of which now covered their back yard. They'd never used a tree service before, so they called a few companies to get an estimate. Two of the contractors provided a written estimate, as well as a timeframe for removal, but it was the third, and last, tree removal service who won their business. And it was all because of a story.

When the homeowner inquired how long it would take and asked about the extent of the services, the gentleman didn't answer the questions, per se. He said, "I just spent yesterday over there in the next block, on Prairie View. Did you see their tree? It had fallen smack dab on top of their house. Rain was gushing in through the roof, and the whole back wall just caved in—worst one I've seen yet from this storm. And the insurance company was pretty stingy—they insisted that whatever I did to remove the tree, I better not create any more damage than was already done. C'mon, the whole wall was destroyed. But I had two crews out there, doubled my equipment, and we lifted that son-of-a-gun straight up in the air and lowered it without so much as touching the house on the way down. And when we cleared the debris away and removed the stump, all in one day—you wouldn't even know there'd ever been a tree there."

The story always sells, and it did in this case. First, the business owner managed to relay a story that happened in their neighborhood, to their neighbors. In doing so, he created characters and a connection. Second, he established an experience or a problem—a wicked storm that caused a great deal of inconvenience and damage—and third, he revealed how he saved the day and what a great job he'd done. He told a story about his service, making it appealing without giving a sales pitch or a bunch of hype. Yes, it is your service that sells. It makes others see you and your business as a part of their solution and their lives. And it's the one thing that will make you stand out above the rest and make you memorable.

What's your story? How did you get started? What inspired you to do what you do? What solutions do you provide? What do you know that the competition doesn't? What experiences have you had? Use this information to tell your story, either in a presentation, a marketing promotion, or when you sit at the table with prospective clients. Share—don't "sell." Whether your story is inspirational, shocking, or hilarious, it will make a bigger, better, and longer impact on your audience than traditional advertising.

Firefighters will always continue to sit around the table and swap stories—they enrich our relationships and enhance our knowledge and careers. The information in them becomes ingrained in and vividly remembered by others. Our stories hold so much value that they become a part of our legacy. And through our legacy, we have the capacity to become a legend.

But, like Nike, if we don't share our unique stories, nobody will know about them.

CONCLUSION

SERVING WITHOUT SELLING IS not a new concept or innovation. Firefighters have employed this strategy since the day our service evolved. It's not a science or a principle taught by Harvard Business School or the National Fire Academy, but I can tell you that it's no less effective in success than extensive training, a good business plan, financial backing, or having a breakthrough product or service.

To serve others is the greatest contribution we can make on their lives, and when we contribute at the highest levels, we don't have to rely on marketing campaigns, hype, or gimmicks to attract business. Instead, we receive sincere attraction from customers and our communities, one that's based on trust, respect, and integrity, not the bottom line.

As a firefighter who is also an entrepreneur, the principles behind serving without selling came to me as a formula for success. After all, if a firefighter can earn the approval and prestige of his or her community without having to plead for it, advertise, or promote him or herself, why shouldn't a business owner or entrepreneur be able to implement the same success strategy? The more I investigated the idea and implemented it in my own business, the more convinced I was that serving is the key behind all success, not selling.

Serving without selling is not a business methodology; it's a proven philosophy. It's not a fad or new trend in the way of doing business—one of many that falls to the wayside in favor of the next greatest idea; it's proven itself throughout time and been at the core of the public's approval and the unblemished reputation that firefighters and other public servants have enjoyed in their communities for generations.

Sales are not the lifeline of a business—sales are the result of the way an entrepreneur runs his business. Service is your lifeline, and without it, you'll find your business in critical condition and in need of life support. When you serve, rather than sell, your business will be healthy, thriving, and filled with abundance.

Follow these guidelines to climb the ladder of success:

- Create core values for your company and live them every day. Ingrain them in your team members and make them non-negotiable. Whether your core values involve putting the customer first, delivering WOW through service (Zappos), or to give sustainably and responsibly (Toms Shoes), make it evident in every interaction and transaction. Did you note that all of those core values reflect serving, not selling?

- Establish your mission, vision for the future, and purpose. The following fire department mission statement embodies each of these in three sentences:

(Mission:) As first responders to fires, medical emergencies, and incidences involving the safety of the public, the mission of the fire department and its members is to protect the safety, lives, and property of those we serve.

(Vision:) Dedicated to saving lives and property, the department makes continual efforts to increased fire prevention and public safety through educational and public awareness programs, and training.

(Purpose:) Consistent delivery of our services in a professional and timely manner provides the foundation and ability of the fire department to make

positive contributions to the residents, businesses, and visitors in our community.

- Define your brand promise. Establish what your service and/or product does for people ... and live by your promise.

Remember Dominos Pizza's promise that you'd get your pizza in 30 minutes or you'd get it free? That promise built their brand into a mega franchise. When they discontinued that promise, business suffered—not because they wouldn't guarantee 30-minute delivery, but because they failed to replace their brand promise with something else that appealed to their customer base. They took away their big brand promise and substituted it with nothing, believing that their pizza could stand on its own. Sales declined, significantly. Their response was epic: Dominos delivered a new promise to listen to their customers and create a better pizza. They even admitted that their pizza sucked in a national campaign. The result? They earned the admiration and respect of their past and future customers, who gave them another shot. Within six months, their sales increased by 16.5 percent—proof that a brand promise is heard loud and clear. Make yours one that your customers will notice—then live up to it.

- Stay authentic. Don't try to be hip if you're not. If your values are based on care and compassion, stick to them. Stay away from trends. Display integrity in your product or service and your relationships with your customers. What happened when Coke strayed away from its authenticity and changed its formula and name to New Coke? Calls to the company more than tripled after the switch, climbing to 1,500 a day. Coke even hired a psychologist to listen in on their hotline. After only three months, the company switched back to their original formula. Coke fans had spoken out so strongly about their desire for Coke to be authentic and not try to be something they weren't that Coke released a statement, saying, "To hear some tell it, April 23, 1985, was a day that will live in marketing infamy... spawning consumer angst the likes of which no business has ever seen."

- Seek mentorship. I can assure you that every firefighter in this great country of ours would not be as skilled, knowledgeable, or respected if it weren't for the fact that a mentor showed him the ropes, shared stories, and provided invaluable guidance and advice. Find someone who can show you the ropes and how to use them, and you'll discover greater success than you could on your own. Two are better than one—firefighters and police officers have partners for a reason. Let a mentor be your partner.

- Collaborate with others. Work together toward a common cause or goal. It's a great way to enhance your strengths and compensate for your weaknesses. Above all, collaboration will earn you a badge of respect and admiration for being cooperative, involved, and participatory, whether it's in your business or in your community.

- Create a business beyond profit. This is critical to avoid being "just another business that will be gone tomorrow." And it encompasses so much. It's the daycare owner who touches hearts and creates lasting memories and relationships with children and their families. It's the guy who owns the pizza restaurant that delivers such an incredible experience that it becomes the go-to place for celebrations and the hangout after Friday night football games. It's the company that goes above and beyond to make a difference in the lives of the people in its community and show they care.

Examples:

In 1999, Amtrak's City of New Orleans train was southbound when it struck a semi-trailer that was hauling steel bars in Bourbonnais, Illinois. Fourteen people died, and 120 people were injured. Employees from the nearby Birmingham Steel Plant rushed to heroically pull passengers from the wreckage, even before first responders arrived. Blain's Farm and Fleet, a large department store nearby, opened its store to accident victims and their families, providing blankets, clothing, shelter, and food. Equipment and employees from Stepan and Mobil chemical plants responded from as far as 40 miles away with vital foam trucks to help firefighters extinguish the blaze. Doctors and nurses rushed from their homes and hospitals to the scene to volunteer to render life-saving aid. These businesses were a part of the community. They didn't charge for their equipment, personnel, or assistance. They didn't ask for reimbursement. They made no profit from their efforts, but instead lost productivity, sales, and profits. And they didn't care. They used this incident to show that their community could depend on them and they were part of it, even if they weren't making a dime.

General Motors recently found out the hard way that when profits become more important than values and products, a business will suffer. Their failure to acknowledge a defect in their ignition switches cost their shareholders more than three billions dollars in just one four-week span. This is evidence that serving the customer with integrity, honesty, and sincerity will result in more profits and loyal customers than focusing on the bottom line. When you focus on value and customer satisfaction, you gain something that you will never be able to put a dollar sign on—respect and trust.

- Understand that everything you do matters. Firefighters know that. It starts long before the alarm rings—we have to train, prepare, clean, organize, and order and stock supplies. From knowing that every second counts in responding to making sure the last ember is extinguished, every move we make contributes to the end result. This goes far beyond carrying out our duties. It's being professional and courageous, while also being compassionate and caring. It pertains to our public image and reputation, the respect we earn in the community, and the contributions we are expected and glad to make in our mission to enhance and save lives and property.

Everything you do matters. Everything. When you hang up your hat at 5 PM, you're not done. Your image and conduct in your neighborhood and community will impact your success. The way you treat your employees and customers will be scrutinized, as will the things you say on social media. You are the face of your business, even when the doors are closed. People will notice and remember the things you say and do—both good and bad. That's also true for the way your employees treat your customers—your employees represent your company, and what they do will reflect on you and your values. Your helpfulness and cooperation, or lack of it, will drive your results. People will patronize your business and buy your product or service if they feel you are worthy of it; it is up to you to establish that worth.

- Have fun. Isn't being an entrepreneur and business owner a lot of work? Sure, it is. So is being a firefighter. We stay up for 24 hours straight, sometimes more. We have to be capable of some very strenuous physical work, and sometimes encounter devastating experiences. Success takes work, and work creates success. But that doesn't mean you can't have fun. You should have fun. Firefighters have fun. We joke around and laugh. We enjoy each other's company. We actually love our jobs and really enjoy going to work. We even enjoy the rush of adrenalin that we get every time we respond to call. You, too, should enjoy what you do and be excited about having the chance to do it for another day.

  Having fun invites creativity, which can be a huge advantage in business success. Don't think so? Look no further than Apple. They're proof that letting your hair down and having some clean fun can't be all bad. It's all about having a positive attitude and creating enjoyable experiences for you, your clients or customers, and your employees. The more your employees enjoy their jobs, the happier they'll be working for you and when interacting with your customers.

I know that every day can be a great day when you're doing something you enjoy. One of my mentors, Greg Reid, says, "Do what you love and love what you do, and you'll have success your whole life through." And he's right. Success isn't measured solely by sales or profits; it's also measured by greater rewards, like respect, job satisfaction and happiness. Those are the rewards firefighters receive, but if we don't enjoy what we are doing and have fun now and then, we'd be doing ourselves, and our communities, a great disservice.

By following the Seven-Rung Success Formula and the principles that represent serving without selling, you'll breathe fresh air into every transaction and interaction. Giving yourself permission to serve, not sell, will become the blood that gives your business life and maintains it for years to come.

You have now received the call to serve. Don't wait for another day—another minute—or another customer to answer it. Answer it with your lights on and sirens blaring. This is your business and every second counts.

Don't give up—GIVE. Don't sell—SERVE.

ABOUT RICHARD BROCCHINI

RICHARD BROCCHINI IS A fire chief officer, leadership thinker, best-selling author, speaker, and entrepreneur.

He is asought-after speaker and trainer in the corporate arena, sharing proven strategies for organizational leadership and superior customer service.

Rich was also the founder and CEO of Third Alarm Coffee and Tea (sold), Author of A Fresh Reminder, co-founder of Life Code Consulting, founder of Modern Time Properties, founder of Fire Life Wellness, creator of Kassel Band and founder of Modern Time DAD…

Rich and his daughter, Sienna Kassel, live in California.

www.richbrocchini.com

48782133R00066

Made in the USA
San Bernardino, CA
18 August 2019